Let the Leaders Steer and the People Drive

Let the Leaders Steer and the People Drive

◆

Performance Coaching Through the PEOPLE Model™

Toni Reece, Neil Annis, and Linda Harland

iUniverse, Inc.

New York Lincoln Shanghai

Let the Leaders Steer and the People Drive
Performance Coaching Through the PEOPLE Model™

iUniverse books may be ordered through booksellers or by contacting:

iUniverse
2021 Pine Lake Road, Suite 100
Lincoln, NE 68512
www.iuniverse.com
1-800-Authors (1-800-288-4677)

The views expressed in this work are solely those of the author and do not necessarily reflect the views of the publisher, and the publisher hereby disclaims any responsibility for them.

ISBN: 978-0-595-42841-0 (pbk)
ISBN: 978-0-595-87179-7 (ebk)

Printed in the United States of America

Contents

Acknowledgements

We would like to thank the following people who have given their support, care, and love through the birthing process of the PEOPLE Academy. We could not have done it without you.

Our families:

Jo, Jack & Toby—Jim, Jesse & Madison—Lynette, Al & baby Grace

Our friends and supporters:

Bonnie, Dawn, Deb, Jonathan Jay, Matt, Peggy, Dick & Jim, Rob, Terri Levine, Terry, Val

And those that have made a significant impact on us and our business:

People Model™ practitioners, Skype, and UK Trade & Investment

Finally, we would like to thank everyone whom we have not mentioned but have helped us on our journey. You know who you are.

Foreword

By Terri Levine, PhD., MCC

This book describes one of the most innovative approaches to performance coaching today. It's a must-have, must-read book for anybody remotely interested in the coaching profession, because it will take coaches from where they are today, to where they will need to be tomorrow. The coaching profession is continually evolving and expanding at a rapid pace. You have to keep up or be left behind.

The PEOPLE Model™ framework takes natural talent, fantastic coaching skills, and fine tunes them so that the coach can now get the full picture of what the client wants their life to be like in all areas. As a coaching system, it provides a powerful framework within which to work, and the coach will be able to link any conversation or exercise to at least one element of the framework. The system provides structure to the coaching sessions, and the coaching becomes more practical and not just "conceptual" for the client.

As a professional Life and Business Coach and the founder of Comprehensive Coaching U and The Coaching Institute, I have coached and trained many people, from all walks of life, all of whom have benefited greatly from learning coaching skills. Not everybody learns coaching skills in order to work as a professional coach. Some people learn coaching skills to enhance their own lives and assist their family and friends, as well as themselves, and there is a large majority who learn coaching to assist them in their existing corporate careers, too.

I have witnessed the rapid growth and expansion of the coaching profession around the globe; I have seen coach training schools come and go and coach training programs change and improve over the years. I have also seen schools change hands and be swallowed up by larger schools, or schools joining forces.

What I have not seen is any indication that coaching and coach training is a fad that will disappear. If anything, it has become more firmly entrenched in our global culture and more acceptable as a profession. Coaching is here to stay.

Over the years, I have been approached with offers to set up my company as a franchise so that others could use my framework and curriculum, but I said no. I have had others approach me to join forces. I said no. I have never been tempted to join forces with any other program because I did not believe they upheld the same standards as those of my own coaching school, and I did not believe they could add anything new or improved to my own curriculum.

Until I met The PEOPLE Academy. And now, my Coaching Institute, together with The PEOPLE Model™, is revolutionizing the Coaching world. And this is also how I can confidently say that these people know what they are talking about, and I speak from first-hand experience of their program.

There are many benefits to using the PEOPLE Model™, but that's why you've bought this book—to discover and learn about them!

To your success!

Terri Levine, PhD., MCC.,
CEO, Comprehensive Coaching U
Speaker and Best Selling Author of *Work Yourself Happy*

Introduction

If you picked this book up because you collect books on business, today's your lucky day! You've just stumbled upon one of the most innovative approaches in the world of performance coaching today. And you've picked a great book to add to your collection!

However, it's more likely that you've picked up this book because, like many people out there, you are looking for ways to bring a group—whether it is a company, individual, team, organization, or community—to the next level.

Maybe you are a business coach, consultant, or trainer looking to offer clients something more than just a skill-based program.

Maybe you have workforce-related issues that demand some solutions. Perhaps goals are not being met, and your business is not as successful as you know it can be.

Perhaps your team doesn't seem motivated, or communication issues are causing bad feelings and poor teamwork.

Or maybe an individual is looking for some motivation, some inspiration, and some information that will help them succeed and improve in all areas of life.

If you fit into any of the above categories, you need the PEOPLE Model™. What is the PEOPLE Model™? In a nutshell, it is a practical and enlightening way of growing a group through its people. That's right. Your people make your business, your team, your organization, or your community. Your people *are* your business, team, organization, or community. How effective they are at their jobs, how inspired they are, how motivated they are, how qualified they are, how happy they are, and how well they work together as a team will all have a direct effect on the success of your organization.

Makes sense when you think about it, right? Of course it does! But while you may understand the premise, figuring out exactly what the issues are, and how to fix them, can be really challenging. So you've figured out your staff are not motivated. Now what? Why isn't my staff motivated, and how do I get them to be? And that's where this book comes in handy. In just a few short hours you'll have all the information and ideas you need to effectively use the PEOPLE Model™ to improve and grow any—that's right, *any*—organization. Best of all, the PEOPLE Model™ makes so much sense and is so easy to use that we guarantee you'll end up asking yourself, "Why didn't I think of that?"

How does the PEOPLE Model™ work? In a nutshell, the PEOPLE Model™ is a performance coaching system with a structure and strategy that promotes progress and growth. Using diagnostic tools and a series of inspiring questions, a practitioner identifies issues and areas of weakness among individuals, teams, and entire companies. The licensed practitioner has access to a business manual and life coaching manual that offer templates, exercises, and resources that can be used in conjunction with the model to make necessary improvements—whether you are a business, a group, or an individual.

The PEOPLE Model™ takes six elements, combines them with three key concepts, and the result is a solution that allows entities, powered by the people, to reach their maximum potential.

The PEOPLE Model™ is a framework, and within that framework is a system. The system can be used for any type of business or group, regardless of size or sector. So while the framework and the system is the same for any organization, the inspiring questions that are asked will change. And this is how the PEOPLE Model™ is easily tailor-made for anyone—business, organization, association, individual, athlete, team. We really mean anyone!

Who Is This Book For?

This book is for anyone—and we really mean anyone—who works within an organization that wants to promote a "working together" culture. Anyone who needs information and ideas on how to grow a business, organization, team, or community through its people will benefit from the few hours it takes to read this book. This book introduces the PEOPLE Model™ as a performance coaching tool that engages the people behind it to build a better organnization. So, who would use the PEOPLE Model™? Quite simply, the PEOPLE Model™ is designed for three key audiences. If you fit into one of them, then the PEOPLE Model™ is for you!

Are you working with a business, providing support to help it grow?

If you are a …

- Experienced coach

- Consultant

- Practitioner

- Trainer

- Business Advisor

… then the PEOPLE Model™ is for you!

Or, are you someone working within an organization, driving its growth?

If you are a …

- Human Resources professional

- Leader

- Manager

- Department head

- Supervisor

… then the PEOPLE Model™ is for you!

This book is for anyone who wants a people focus in their organization, as well as a business-focused workforce. This book is for people involved in big organizations, as well as people involved in small organizations. As a matter of fact, one of the unique things about the PEOPLE Model™ is that it is non-prescriptive. What do we mean by this? We mean it works well in all sizes and types of organizations, and compliments any and all improvement strategies. It is a boundary-free model with no beginning and no end.

There is also a third key audience that can benefit by the PEOPLE Model™. And this is anyone involved in life coaching. The PEOPLE Model™ as a life coaching system helps the client see what they want their life to be like and how their wants and dreams fit into that vision. That's right. While the PEOPLE Model™ is a great business development resource, we've mentioned it works well for non-business related groups such as boards, sports teams, volunteer organizations, and life coaches. How can a method that works for a business also be good for a sports team? Because the success of both depends on its people. But the model will work for both, because the questions you ask for a business will be quite different from those you will ask for a sports team. We'll get into some examples of questions later, and you'll understand how non-prescriptive the PEOPLE Model™ is. It bears repeating that the PEOPLE Model™ is a framework, and within that framework lies a system.

What You Can Expect From This Book

In the few short hours it takes to read this book, you'll come to understand how the PEOPLE Model™ provides a simple yet powerful approach to complex issues of performance management and process improvement. Whether you are a business that isn't reaching its productivity goals, an association that feels like it is stuck in a rut, or a sports team that just can't make it to the next level despite tons of talent, the inspiring questions will help you diagnose the root of the problem. You'll come up with a list of barriers to performance, and through something called "task coaching," you'll figure out as a group how to break those barriers down. In the end you will create a culture of continuous improvement that will eventually lead you to the results you desire.

- By now you are probably wondering what the acronym PEOPLE stands for. Don't worry—we're going to tell you! All you need to know right now is that the letters PEOPLE stand for six elements that provide the framework for the model. You work within that framework to pinpoint issues, come up with ideas to improve the issue, and make positive changes.

- You'll understand why the PEOPLE Model™ works, and how you can use it to grow and improve any organization.

- You'll learn how to use innovative diagnostic tools to identify organizational and individual needs.

- You'll understand how three key components—inspiration, exploration, and facilitation—are used within each element to ensure the model's success.

- You'll have a clear understanding of the benefits businesses and organizations that use the PEOPLE model™ enjoy.

- You'll realize how the PEOPLE Model™ is different from other offerings on the market.

- You'll learn all about becoming a licensed PEOPLE Model™ practitioner.

- You'll be in possession of a rich set of tools that will allow you to "explore" and improve the group environment.

- Life coaches will be able to help their clients meet their individual goals.

- You'll be motivated, inspired, and educated to change your business or organization! And you'll be able to help others become motivated, inspired, and educated as well.

Who Are We, and Why Should You Listen to Us?

You are probably wondering who we are and why you should listen to us. Well, we are Toni Reece, Neil Annis, and Linda Harland, owners of the PEOPLE Academy. What is the PEOPLE Academy? It is a new, international business with offices in the United States, United Kingdom, and Australasia. It came about when two organizations decided to merge their skills, knowledge, and experience—more than 50 years experience combined, by the way!—of the founding partners, which resulted in the development of the PEOPLE Model™. What we saw when we took a good look around were plenty of excellent skill-based training programs for coaches, but very little in the way of development training. The PEOPLE Academy saw a need for growth and development in performance improvement. We felt that none of the existing models gave a fully comprehensive tool that could easily be applied in a business-focused context.

So that became our mission, and what a mission it was! We set out to develop a sophisticated, logical, and impacting international model that could provide a practical, people-focused approach to performance development. Did we do it? You bet! It was a long and interesting journey that had each of us flying across the world to meet, brainstorm, and develop the concept and framework of the model. There was some soul searching and a lot of exploration before the model evolved. It was a bit like having three mad scientists locked in a room and throwing all the chemicals together, but when we finally had it, we knew it!

And now that we have it, we want to share it so that others can be successful. This book, an enlightening and practical resource on how to build your organization through your people, is just one of the steps we are taking to spread the word and make a difference for companies, and employees, everywhere. We are already in the process of licensing many talented, qualified PEOPLE Model™ practitioners to help us help you. And we're already seeing explosive growth in different sectors and in different parts of the world. After all, when something is good, it just works! We are glad you have chosen to join us on this journey. Turn the page, and let's begin!

PART I
Let the People Drive

1

The Power of PEOPLE

Before we go any further, we wanted to talk just a bit about the title of this book, *Let the Leaders Steer and the People Drive*. If you can understand this premise as it relates to business or any organization that requires groups of people to interact, then you can understand the whole idea behind the PEOPLE Model™. When Toni Reece, our American founder, worked in the quality department of a large international battery company, she made a startling discovery. Sure, the company was focused on Continuous Quality Improvement, otherwise known as CQI. And everything was very process-oriented when it came to quality control. But the employees, from the manager to the person on the factory floor, often followed directions without knowing why they were doing what they were doing. The importance of what they were doing—and how it fit into the overall success of the company—was completely lost on them. In most cases, the employee was not able to link what they were doing to the company objectives. So how invested do you think such an employee is in his or her task? How invested would you be if you had no idea why you were doing something? Not very, right?

The PEOPLE Model™ is designed for the company with the employee who has been on the factory floor for 35 years without so much as one person asking them what they have learned or what they know about their job. It's designed for the company whose sales rep is trying to think outside the box, but doesn't know what the "right" box is. Are these workers using their talents and abilities to do the best job they can do? Of course not. And what's the end result? The company as a whole also isn't meeting its full potential.

The PEOPLE Model™ is designed for organizations that are having communication problems. It is designed for organizations that are not consistently reaching production goals. It is designed for organizations with management issues, training and development issues, motivation issues, and ownership issues. It is for organizations that want to build trust, are concerned with continuous improvement, want to learn how to manage change, or need to come up with an action plan. The PEOPLE Model™ is for individuals, teams, and organizations. And the beauty of the model is that it benefits all of them, individually, while benefiting them as a whole. The PEOPLE Model™ is an improvement system based on people-focused performance. When people are linked to the goals and outcomes of a company, they are able to reach their highest potential. And when that happens, the company reaches its highest potential as well.

The PEOPLE Model™ engages people. It uses their power to uncover issues—to find out what's blocking the power to produce—and makes them own the outcome. In a nutshell, the PEOPLE Model™ works by inspiring workers to determine what needs to be changed within the organizational structure in order for the company to meet its objectives and goals. Strengths and weaknesses are defined, often using one of the many diagnostic tools available through the PEOPLE Model.™ Workers then explore different ways to effect positive change. And what's the final step? They then facilitate those changes. Inspiration—exploration—facilitation—it's all part of the PEOPLE process.

Why the PEOPLE Model™ is Different

There are a lot of business coaching models out there. Some of them are really great! Many of these models teach specific skills like leadership skills, management skills, and even job-related skills. And don't get us wrong, it's important for workers to have the appropriate job skills. There is certainly a place for these types of programs.

Neil Annis and Linda Harland worked together in the United Kingdom in a Training and Enterprise Council, where their job was to ensure that people had the right skills to be employable. But attending a program in London with the Pacific Institute, where they eventually became practitioners, made them understand how important cognitive issues such as self-esteem and motivation are to employee—and ultimately business—success. As practitioners who eventually struck out on a business venture together, they became integral partners to people's self-discovery. They watched, awe-struck, as people changed their own lives with the tools they gave them. They realized that in order for a business to successfully change anything—whether it was economic, technological, or structural—people had to change their mindsets first. It was an important realization for both of them, and one that would certainly have an influence upon the PEO-PLE Model™.

So when we all—Toni, Neil, and Linda—came together we had lots of experience in business improvement. And we all believed that while it's a no-brainer that employees have the right skills to excel at their jobs, building skills is often not enough. Even the most skilled worker in the world isn't going to benefit the company if his idea of what is expected of him doesn't gel with the manager's idea of what is expected of him. When things go awry in a company—as an example let's say communication breaks down—management tends to focus on that skill. In this case, that "skill" is communication. What is the company's course of action? In many cases they bring in a business coach to build the communication skills of the parties involved.

In the end, is the company any better off? If they haven't identified the reasons for the communication issues, then allowed the workers to take part in fixing the issue, then the answer is an emphatic "no." And that's where the PEOPLE Model™ is a little different. We've mentioned before that this is not a one-size-fits-all program. This isn't a "course" on how to improve this or that. Instead, it is a framework that allows employees—that's right, employees—to determine areas of strength and weakness and to come up with a roadmap on how to run their organization more effectively.

We have a strategy that we call Inspiration—Exploration—Facilitation. We've mentioned it before. How does it work? Well, using the six elements that form the acronym PEOPLE (and don't worry, we're almost to the point of telling you what they are!) the model asks questions to "inspire" people to find the areas of strength and weakness. It then gets them to "explore" ideas and options for improving their situation. Finally, it gives them the tools to "facilitate" the change.

Pretty simple, right? We think so. As a matter of fact we've designed the framework and strategy so that people simply "get it." It's simple, it's logical, and it's incredibly effective.

It Really Does Work

Before we go into detail regarding the PEOPLE Model™, let's go over why it works:

- The PEOPLE Model™ is driven by people-focused performance. Remember, a company is only as good as the people behind it!

- People are involved in the goals and objectives of the company, and understand why they are doing the jobs they are doing, as well as how important they are.

- The PEOPLE Model™ is a model without a beginning or an end. It has no boundaries, and allows the practitioner to marry his or her skills with a business development framework.

- The PEOPLE Model™ is non-prescriptive. It works for businesses in all sectors, of all types and sizes. It works for boards, associations, sports teams, and just about any other group of people with goals in mind.

- The model engages the organization, and because of its format takes the personalities out of issues and makes them non-confrontational.

- The PEOPLE Model™ is designed to inspire the right thinking, explore options of change, and guide and facilitate to remove barriers.

- The PEOPLE Model™ framework is simple, logical, yet very effective in its simplicity.

- With the PEOPLE Model™, workers own their job roles. They ask three important questions: What are my responsibilities? Who am I responsive to? What is my accountability?

- The PEOPLE Model™ is designed to allow leaders to steer the company to the next level, while letting the people drive!

The PEOPLE Model™ As a Business Opportunity

If you are a business coach, trainer, consultant, life coach or other specialist who wants to take your own business to the next level, then becoming a PEOPLE Model™ practitioner might be the right choice for you.

For starters, this book is designed to give you a good understanding of the model and how you can incorporate it into your business. Just like the PEOPLE Model™ itself, the opportunity for a practitioner to use the model with new or existing clients has no boundaries! It's possible to tailor the model to address an endless variety of challenges, and because it is non-prescriptive you can tailor it to businesses and organizations of all different sizes and types. Quite simply, the PEOPLE Model™ is a complete business!

What are some other reasons you should consider using the PEOPLE Model™?

- The PEOPLE Model™ is a clear strategy for growth, whether we are talking about a business, an organization, a team, or an individual.

- The PEOPLE Model™ translates easily between practitioners, business leaders, managers, and teams.

- The PEOPLE Model™ can be used with existing clients to drive deeper into the heart of the business.

- The PEOPLE Model™ makes a positive difference!

Now that you know the basic premise behind the PEOPLE Model™, how it's different, and why it works, it's time to get into more detail. In Chapter Two we'll finally tell you what that acronym stands for. We'll explain the six elements and introduce you to the model's diagnostic tools. We'll tell you what a business using the PEOPLE Model™ can expect to experience along the way, as well as some of the outcomes and benefits that businesses can expect to enjoy. By the end of Chapter Two you'll know exactly how the PEOPLE Model™ works!

2

The PEOPLE Model™

Now that you've got a pretty good understanding of what the PEOPLE Model™ is designed to do, you are probably wondering what those letters stand for! Well, the letters provide the framework of the entire model. They stand for:

Performance

Efficacy

Ownership

Possibilities

Linkage

Evidence

Finally! Aren't you glad we finally let you in on what the acronym stands for?

Chances are, you probably know what all of these words mean. After all, they are fairly common words used in everyday conversation. However, these six little words are designed to facilitate a company's journey of discovery and achievement in a big, big way.

As a matter of fact, one of the reason why the PEOPLE Model™ is so successful is that it uses language that just about anyone can comprehend.

Consider the Webster's New Universal Unabridged Dictionary definition of each element:

Performance, n. 1. The act of performing; execution; accomplishment.

2. operation or functioning, usually with regard to effectiveness, as of an airplane.

3. something done or performed; deed or feat.

4. a formal exhibition of skill or talent, as a play, a musical program, etc.; a show.

Efficacy, n, power to produce effects or intended results; effectiveness.

Ownership, n, 1. The state or fact of being an owner.

2. proprietorship; legal right of possession; legal or just claim or title.

Possibilities, n, pl, that which is possible; a thing which may possibly happen, be, or exist.

Linkage, n, 1. A linking or being linked.

2. a series of system of links; especially a series of connecting rods for transmitting power or motion.

Evidence, n, 1. The condition of being evident.

2. something that makes another thing evident; indication; sign.

3. something that tends to prove; ground for belief.

Six simple words that, when properly used, can change the culture of your business or organization.

So, how are these six elements used?

The first step is to diagnose the issue, or the issues, that a company or organization is facing. These issues may be evident, or they may be somewhat unclear. If they are unclear, the practitioner may choose to use one of the PEOPLE Academy's diagnostic tools. After diagnosing the issue, or issues, that a company is facing, those issues are plugged into one or more of the elements. Let's say, to take a specific example, that production goals are not being met at a t-shirt factory.

We know what the problem is. Now under what element would you plug it in?

Well, in this case there are several elements under which this particular problem could be placed. And you may choose to place it under several or just one. Perhaps you have determined that production goals are not being met because workers are not performing as managers expect them to. Perhaps they are not really clear on their job descriptions, or how their performance affects the bottom line of the business. So for the sake of this exercise, let's choose Ownership.

Under this element you would ask the workers several questions. What are your responsibilities? Who are you responsive to? Where are you responsive? What is your accountability? Often, managers and leaders don't take the time to furnish the answers for employees because they either feel that telling employees what to do goes against their particular management "style," or they feel that employees shouldn't need to be told what to do. But often workers who don't understand what they are supposed to be doing, or why they are doing what they are doing, are perceived as lazy and unmotivated. By asking three key questions, the root of the problem is determined. "A ha!" a manager might say, after such an exercise. "My workers aren't lazy and unmotivated after all. They simply don't understand what is expected of them. And all along I've been disciplining them and wondering why it hasn't been working!"

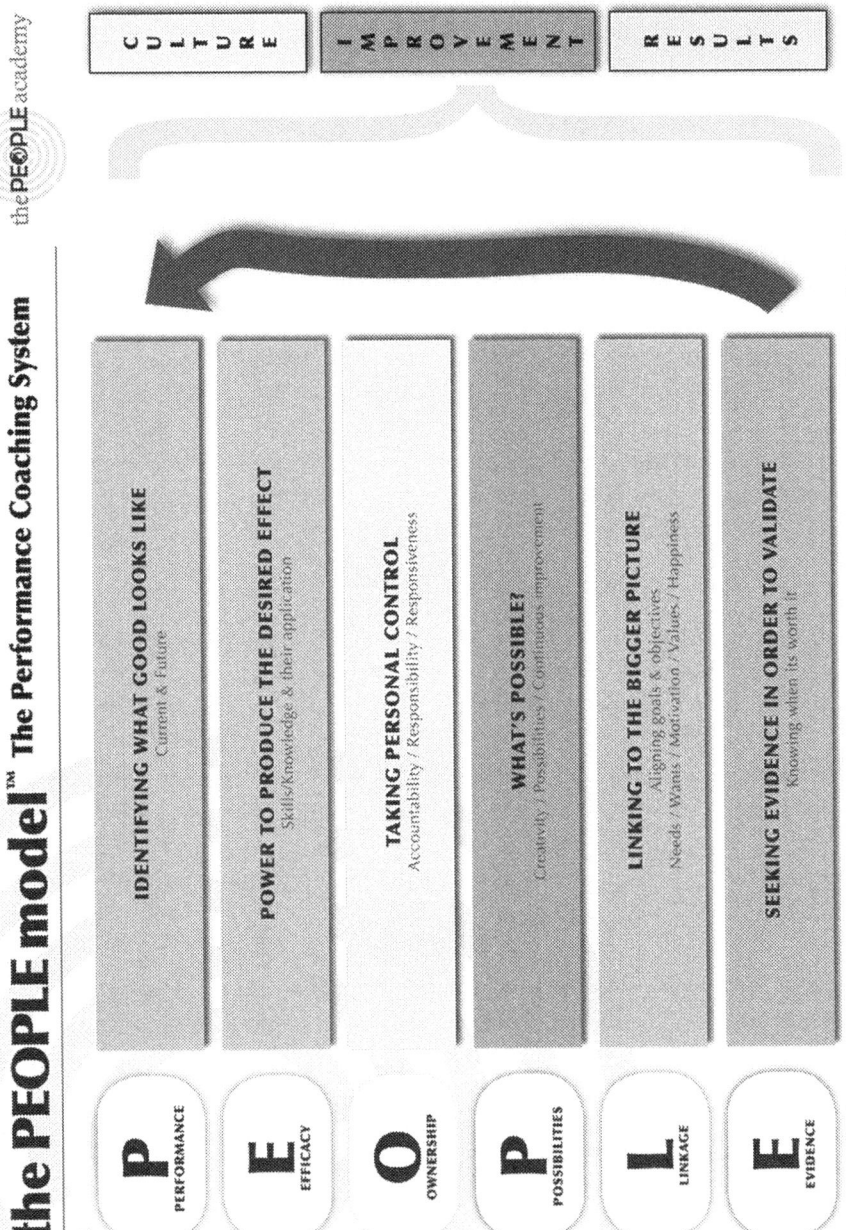

the PEOPLE model™ The Performance Coaching System

P PERFORMANCE — **IDENTIFYING WHAT GOOD LOOKS LIKE** Current & Future

E EFFICACY — **POWER TO PRODUCE THE DESIRED EFFECT** Skills/Knowledge & their application

O OWNERSHIP — **TAKING PERSONAL CONTROL** Accountability / Responsibility / Responsiveness

P POSSIBILITIES — **WHAT'S POSSIBLE?** Creativity / Possibilities / Continuous improvement

L LINKAGE — **LINKING TO THE BIGGER PICTURE** Aligning goals & objectives Needs / Wants / Motivation / Values / Happiness

E EVIDENCE — **SEEKING EVIDENCE IN ORDER TO VALIDATE** Knowing when its worth it

CULTURE IMPROVEMENT RESULTS

the PE●PLE academy

But it isn't until Inspiration—Exploration—Facilitation are introduced that the model really begins to be successful. In fact, Inspiration—Exploration—Facilitation™ are the embedded strategy that makes the PEOPLE Model™ work. How are they used?

As people experience a momentum toward their goal they become "inspired" to take on more and more. Years of experience have proven that once that starts to happen, the old adage, "The whole is better than the sum of its parts," begins to ring true. What is behind the inspiration? It is the questions that are asked that really inspire groups to get excited about change. We are going to talk about some of those questions in a moment, specifically, what kinds of questions you might ask under each element.

Once people are inspired to begin thinking differently and effecting change, they can begin to "explore" all the ways of reaching their goals. The PEOPLE Model™ has a set of tools that enable people to explore their business more deeply.

Finally, as people begin to better understand their organization and what it's going to take to reach their goals, they are able to come up with a plan to "facilitate" action in order to meet those goals.

And there you have, in a nutshell, the PEOPLE Model™. Simple, isn't it? Well, we told you so! The model is made up of six elements—Performance, Efficacy, Ownership, Possibilities, Linkage, and Evidence; and three key components: Inspiration—Exploration—Facilitation. Use them together, and you've got a unique, innovative system that puts people in power!

Now that you realize how understandable yet logical the system is, we want to talk a bit more in detail about each of the six elements. Once you understand each of them in more detail, you'll have a better understanding of how to use the model as a whole.

The Six Elements

The six elements are easy to remember, because they spell PEOPLE. And what is this model all about? People, of course! Remember, you needn't plug your issue into all six elements in order for the model to work its magic. In fact, in many cases the issue at hand will fall under only one element.

Performance.

Performance is identifying what good looks like, now and in the future. Ask any company what their biggest challenge is, and their answer is likely to be performance.

So, how does the practitioner help the organization, individual, or company meet the top challenge of performance? By asking the right questions to determine the company's needs. These would include questions like,

- "What does good look like currently?"

- "What does good look like for the team and individuals?"

- "What does good look like for the performance of product, team, and individuals?"

- "What should good look like for all of the above in the future?"

It's important to note that the practitioner will stay out of the debate regarding what good looks like. Instead, he will guide the organization, and the individuals within that organization, to the answers that are right for them.

There are two important concepts that the practitioner will try to promote under the Performance Element. The first is the concept of "wiggle room." This concept will allow for some room to modify the path or position of the organization, team, or individual on the way toward the goal. After all, there is rarely one route on any journey!

The second concept the practitioner will promote is "two sets of lenses." What does this mean? It means that thoughts, ideas, etc. should not be dealt with in a one-dimensional manner. In other words, the overall objective of the company may be very different from the overall objective of the individual. It's important that both the company and the individual acknowledge and respect an alternate way of looking at things.

Performance: Questions to Inspire
- "What does good look like currently?"

- "What does good look like for the team and individuals?"

- "What does good look like for the performance of product, team, and individuals?"

- "What should good look like for all of the above in the future?"

Example: The Manic Morning Coffee Company is keeping up with the heavy demand for its flavored coffees, but is having issues with quality control. Specifically, customers are not happy with the consistency of the flavors, which is resulting in returned coffee, and loss of profits. The crew who manufactures the coffee is well-trained, but management is frustrated and chalks the problem up to sloppy errors as a result of lack of motivation and care. The crew, however, feels like they are doing the best they can. After all, sales of Manic Monday flavored coffee have tripled in the last year, and they are doing their best to meet demand. So what happens when the PEOPLE Model™ practitioner asks both management and employees what good looks like?

Management says good looks like rising profits as a result of steady sales, which can only be realized if the coffee is properly flavored and customers are satisfied.

Employees, on the other hand, feel that meeting demand is what good looks like. They have absolutely no idea that their errors, which are a result of trying to keep up with heavy demand, affected the bottom line.

The solution? Well, hopefully both sides employ the concept of the "two sets of lenses" and can see where each side is coming from. In fact, both meeting demand and meeting customer satisfaction are integral to the company's bottom line. Now that they have a goal in common and are inspired to make some changes, it is up to them to explore different ways of making that goal come to fruition. Once they've come up with a solution—together—they can facilitate their plan keeping in mind, of course, that they'll need a little "wiggle room" to allow for changes and detours along the way.

In the end, everyone wins.

Efficacy

The second element of the PEOPLE Model™ is Efficacy. What exactly is efficacy? It is the power to produce the desired effect for the business. Think about the dictionary definition for a second. Efficacy is how effective something is.

During this stage, the practitioner may choose to use one of the PEOPLE Academy's diagnostic tools to facilitate the identification of barriers that are blocking the power to produce. If you are wondering what those diagnostic tools are, don't worry, we'll fill you in. In the meantime, in addition to the diagnostic tools, questions the practitioner might ask to inspire the group might include:

- "What is getting in the way of the desired performance?"

- "What are the differences between effectiveness and commitment?"

- "What habits, attitudes, beliefs, and expectations affect the power to produce the desired goal?"

Again, these questions are meant to inspire people at all levels to think about what, indeed, is blocking the power to produce.

Efficacy: Questions to Inspire
- "What is getting in the way of the desired performance?"

- "What are the differences between effectiveness and commitment?"

- "What habits, attitudes, beliefs, and expectations affect the power to produce the desired goal?"

Example:

A local golf club has watched its membership dwindle. And they can't understand why. After all, their membership drive has been more or less the same for years. The volunteer staff are working harder than ever to keep membership up. This year, because of dwindling capital, the golf club is faced with closing its doors.

The members of the board sit down with a PEOPLE Model™ practitioner to try to figure out why their plan of action is no longer effective. They are certainly working harder than ever, but something seems wrong.

The team sits down to discuss barriers, and deals with them one by one to find a way to meaningful change. It is determined that the board understands its job and certainly doesn't need to be told what to do—after all, they've been doing this for years. They are also competent, committed, and have plenty of tools to get the members in the door in terms of time, budget, and people.

So what's up? The practitioner does an exercise that looks at invisible barriers, specifically habits, attitudes, beliefs, and expectations.

And all of these are challenged. The group has an inspiring, dynamic conversation about who its members have been, and who its members should be. Traditionally the club has offered one level of membership. But changing family dynamics mean that in order to continue to attract members, the club might have to be flexible and come up with several different tiers of membership to accommodate a more diverse group of people. If they want the club to survive, they may have to change their attitudes and beliefs about their membership.

Ownership

Ownership means taking personal control of a situation. It means understanding how accountability, responsibility, and responsiveness apply to ownership. And it means being responsible for oneself. We can tell you quite honestly, there isn't an organization out there that isn't affected by some kind of ownership issue! It happens to all kinds of businesses, in all sectors and in all sizes. Some ownership issues go from individual to individual, while others go from individual to team. Still others go from team to team.

Let's talk about the three main keywords that make up ownership:

Accountable: If you are accountable, it means that you are liable to account for your actions, and are obliged to accept responsibility.

Responsible: If you are responsible, it means that you are able to make moral or rational decisions on your own, and are therefore answerable for your behavior. It means you are able to be trusted and depended upon.

Responsive: If you are responsive, it means that you are answering or replying, and that you are readily reacting.

The practitioner can use the ownership element to inspire clients by asking questions like:

- "What does ownership mean to you/your company?"

- "Do you own what good looks like?"

- "What is the difference between accountability, responsibility, and responsiveness in teams and individuals?"

- "What does it mean to give up accountability?"

By helping to identify ownership issues, the practitioner can facilitate an understanding of how these issues are affecting an individual, a team, or maybe even the company as a whole.

Example:

The owner of a public relations firm needs to get some energy and passion back into the organization. She can't quite put her finger on why the motivation is missing, but she notices that her employees rush out the door every day at exactly 5 p.m.—and that's after watching the clock since lunch! She would love for her employees to be as passionate about her business as she is. But how can she accomplish this?

Enter the licensed PEOPLE Model™ practitioner, who knows that lack of passion can result from lack of ownership. Using the PEOPLE Model™, the practitioner helps uncover the sources of energy loss, and facilitates reconnecting people to the sense of the business purpose. Involvement in the company comes from understanding the business needs and the role the people make in that plan of needs. Helping people see where they belong and where they make a positive difference in their job, team, or organization will help regain energy and passion.

Ownership: Questions to Inspire
- "What does ownership mean to you/your company?"

- "Do you own what good looks like?"

- "What is the difference between accountability, responsibility, and responsiveness in teams and individuals?"

- "What does it mean to give up accountability?"

Possibilities

What is possible? The Possibilities element of the PEOPLE Model™ explores things like creativity, possibilities, and continuous improvement. It examines the potential for favorable or interesting results.

The practitioner might ask questions like,

- "How willing is the company to think about possibilities?"

- "What is self-talk, team talk, and organizational talk?"

- "Are there perception problems?"

- "What is in place to sustain progress and potential?"

- "What is happening to impact progress and potential?"

The Possibilities element is the one that allows people to dream! That's right! This is the time when the practitioner can facilitate possibilities thinking by asking workers to dream about what the company can do, or what needs to be created so that the company can achieve its dream and turn them into actions. In a nutshell, dreaming + creating = action!

At this point the practitioner might use one of the diagnostic tools that would bring to light the issues that are impacting the company's ability to create and dream. The Possibilities element is also a good time for the practitioner to explore the readiness for change, and identify how resilient the client is, or needs to be.

Example:

A salsa company has noticed an increase in company complaints, a result of quality errors, in recent months. A PEOPLE Model™ practitioner is brought in to help address the problem.

Using the diagnostic tools, the practitioner helps the staff come to the conclusion that the customer complaints are a result of business practices. So under the Possibilities element, the practitioner helps the company see what is possible in terms of how they approach their current business practices, using the available resources, people, and facility that they currently have. Using inspiring questions, the staff are encouraged to think outside the box in terms of their business practices, and then facilitates a course of action for improving those business practices.

Possibilities: Questions to Inspire
- "How willing is the company to think about possibilities?"

- "What is self-talk, team talk, and organizational talk?"

- "Are there perception problems?"

- "What is in place to sustain progress and potential?"

- "What is happening to impact progress and potential?"

Diagnostic Tools Demystified

Okay, we've talked a lot about diagnostic tools. So here's a brief explanation of each diagnostic tool and its intended purpose. Diagnostic tools and how to use them are covered in detail in the PEOPLE Model's™ practitioner manual.

- Task Coaching Sessions. These are coaching sessions focused on an individual or team to identify what gets in the way of good performance.

- Perception Gap. www.PerceptionGap.com is an online staff survey that seeks input from everyone on what works well and what works less well in their organization. Perception Gap produces a significant report from input provided by staff for leaders to review with their PEOPLE Model™ practitioner.

• Development Wheels. This diagnostic tool allows clients to rate satisfaction in several different areas, and identifies areas that need to be worked on. The exercise also allows those involved to understand the skills and attributes needed to fill the gaps.

Linkage

The fifth element of the PEOPLE Model™ is linkage. Linkage refers to linking to the big picture. It is how personal, team, and organizational objectives are aligned at the end of the day!

What are some questions a practitioner might ask to get the Linkage element flowing?

• "When do you start to think about linking employees to business objectives?"

• "How important are attitudes, behavior, and values as links?"

• "What are the teams' roles and responsibilities to linkage?"

Again, one of several diagnostic tools might be used, along with the answers to the inspiring questions, to identify gaps in the chain.

Example:

A local football team has won the State Championship for the last ten years, but now has two significant competitors that are not only gaining, but seem to have an edge this season. The State Champions want their edge back!

The PEOPLE Model™ gives the team a framework for an internal review of the team's processes and thinking. Under the Linkage element, the team is able to discover how athletes are linked to the team's goals. The team's attitude, behavior, and values are explored as links, and the team's roles and responsibilities to linkage are examined.

These exercises will help the team identify any gaps in the chain, and address them in a way that gets them on top again.

Linkage: Questions to Inspire
- "When do you start to think about linking employees to business objectives?"

- "How important are attitudes, behavior, and values as links?"

- "What are the teams' roles and responsibilities to linkage?"

Evidence

The final element in the PEOPLE Model™ is Evidence. This is the stage at which you seek evidence in order to validate. There is a validation point in any process. It is the point at which you ask yourself if what you are working on is truly working.

The concept used to inspire workers at this point is called the invisible obvious. What is an invisible obvious? Well, company mission statements and company values are great examples. Chances are, a company's mission statement is hanging on the wall for everyone to see. But, is it invisible to employees? In other words, do employees understand the statement? Does it resonate with them? Or, let's take company values as another example of the invisible obvious. Values might include communication, accountability, or customer delight. But is there evidence that these values are working? It might be obvious to managers or leaders, but not so obvious to other employees. The goal of this element is to provide the evidence that validates that what you are working on is actually working. In other words, making the invisible, visible!

Evidence: Questions to Inspire
- Do you measure the return on investment?

- What is the impact of your activities or improvement?

- When do you know what you are working on is truly working?

3

Why the PEOPLE Model™ is NOT Just For Businesses

The PEOPLE Model™ is not just for businesses. Because its unique framework, and the system within it, involve people, The PEOPLE Model™ works well for any association, group, team, or individual that wants to better its performance and reach goals. The PEOPLE Model™ works well for:

- Boards

- Associations

- Volunteer organizations

- Sports teams

- Individuals

In a nutshell, the PEOPLE Model™ works well for any entity that relies on people to be successful.

To understand how non-prescriptive the PEOPLE Model™ is, and why it is successful in a wide variety of areas, let's look at some examples. Again, we'll drill down under each element to show you exactly how the PEOPLE Model™ works in certain situations.

Performance

Let's say that a business is having a particular performance issue. The barrier has been discovered using one of the PEOPLE Model's diagnostic tools such as task coaching, the development wheels, or Perception Gap.

If the PEOPLE Model™ practitioner were dealing with a business, he or she might ask powerful and inspiring coaching questions such as:

- What is the vision for the organization?

- Why does this organization exist?

- If your organization did not exist, what would be the impact to customers/staff/the community?

- Take me through what good performance looks like for the organization/team/department/site/individual role. For this particular question the practitioner might look at such areas as:

  —Finances

  —Outputs

  —Efficiency

  —Return On Investment

  —Volume

  —Widgets

  —Key performance indicators

  —Effectiveness

  —Standards

  —Image

  —Pricing

  —Units Sold

  —Orders

- Who is responsible for what?

- Take me through what you see good performance looking like in the future for the organization/team/site/department/individual.

- What gets in the way of good performance for the organization/team/department/site/individual role?

- How do you know?

- What do you think others (Leaders/Managers/Staff) think gets in the way of good performance in the organization/team/department/site/individual?

- How would they know?

How does your good compare to that of your competitors?

These questions will inspire leaders, managers, and workers to think about if and how they are currently meeting their performance goals, and how they would like to meet such goals in the future. They can then move on to exploring ways to meet their goals. The next step is facilitation. What does this mean? It means making things happen! That's right. Once the group knows what good looks like, and what they want good to look like, they come up with a plan and put that plan in motion. This creates a culture of continual improvement.

And now we want to show you how this culture can be promoted in just about any group that depends upon people to keep it going. This is great news for life coaches, coaches of sports teams, people who lead volunteer groups, and board members who want to see their groups enjoy optimal success.

Let's say you are a PEOPLE Model™ practitioner who has been called in to help a local women's hockey team win the national championship. The team in question has advanced to the national championships every year for the past four years but can't seem to bring home the trophy. Everyone agrees it is not because of lack of talent.

How could a PEOPLE Model™ practitioner help this team reach its goals?

First of all, just like with a business, one or more of the diagnostic tools might be used. In this case, let's assume Task Coaching is used. The practitioner will help the team discover its barriers to performance by asking them to individually state what they perceive the barriers are, remove duplicates, and then rank them in order of importance.

The PEOPLE Model™ practitioner will then ask the team questions to inspire them to think about change. And when we say team we mean everyone that is involved with the team, from the coaches to the goalie.

Questions might include:

- What is the overall goal of this team?

- Why does this team exist?

- If this team did not exist, how would it change your lives as individuals? Why do you play on this team, and what do you hope to get out of it?

- If this team did not exist, what would be the impact on the community?

- What does good performance currently look like for the team? The practitioner may ask the participants to look at individual areas such as:

    —Wins and losses

    —Improvement

    —Team cohesiveness

    —Attitude

    —Coaching

    —Commitment

    —Skill set

- What would you like good performance to look like in the future?

- Who is responsible for what?

- What gets in the way of peak performance for this team?

- How do you know?

- What do you think others (coaches/spectators) think gets in the way of good performance for this team?

- How would they know?

- How does your good compare to that of your competitors?

Whether you are a PEOPLE Model™ practitioner working with a Fortune 500 company or a PEOPLE Model™ practitioner working with a local hockey team, the model is exactly the same. It is just the questions that have changed. In both cases, the idea is to get the people involved with both organizations to think about what good performance looks like to them. The questions inspire them to think about what good is and what good should be. This inspiration leads to the exploration of ideas, and finally to facilitation to make goals a reality.

We want to keep drilling under each element to show you the versatility of the model. We've already done Performance; let's do the rest.

Efficacy

A PEOPLE Model™ practitioner working with a business might ask the following questions under the Efficacy element:

- How is it possible for you to achieve your goals?

- Talk me through the learning, training, and development that takes place within the business.

- What does coaching mean to you/the business?

- How would coaching best improve this business?

- How do teams and individuals unblock their thinking when they get stuck?

- Tell me about the esteem of the business.

- How do you think your competitors see this business?

- How would you want them to see it?

- How do you think your staff's families see this business?

- How would you want them to see it?

- How do you think the community sees this business?

- How would you want them to see it?

- Do people have the skills required to do the job to the standards required?

- How do you know when there are skill gaps within the business?

- What is the self-belief of the business?

Now we would like to give an example of what kinds of questions, using the same exact model, would be asked for a foundation made up of volunteers who go to third-world countries to build schoolhouses. What kinds of questions would a PEOPLE Model™ practitioner ask to ensure that the organization was effective?

Questions might include:

- How is it possible for you to achieve your goals?

- What skill set, learning, training, and development must your volunteers possess in order for this foundation to be effective?

- How do volunteers unblock their thinking when they get stuck?

- Tell me about the esteem of the foundation.

- How do you think friends, family, and people in the community see this foundation?

- How would you like them to see it?

- How do you think the people you help see this foundation?

- How would you like them to see it?

- Do your volunteers have the skills they need to help the foundation accomplish its goals?

- Do your volunteers have the tools and resources needed to help the foundation accomplish its goals?

- How do you know when there are skill gaps with volunteers?

- How do you know when there are commitment gaps with volunteers?

- How do you know when there are resource gaps at the foundation?

- What is the self-belief of the foundation?

Questions such as these will allow the foundation to examine its effectiveness, and to explore ways of being more effective. Areas such as resources and tools, commitment level of the volunteers, skill set, and how the foundation perceives itself and is perceived in the community, will be discussed. The questions will inspire the foundation to brainstorm and explore ideas that will help them be as effective as they want to be. The final step of facilitation allows them to put their plan into motion. The end result will be a foundation whose environment and culture supports continual effectiveness in their goal toward building school-houses in third-world countries.

Ownership

A PEOPLE Model™ practitioner working with a business might ask the following questions under the Ownership element:

- Talk me through where the business/site/people/teams/individuals own their performance.

- Tell me where you see people are responsible for the outputs they produce.

- Where would you improve personal accountability?

- How?

- Where would you improve personal responsibility?

- How?

- Where would you improve personal responsiveness?

- How?

- What would be different here if people were more accountable?

- What would be different here if people were even more responsible?

- What would be different if people were even more responsive?

Using different questions but the same model, a life coach might use the Ownership element to help an individual achieve overall success in his or her life. Used in life coaching, the PEOPLE Model™ allows clients to see where their actions, emotions, relationships, finances, and career all fit into the life they have. In the end, the client will easily be able to see where they need to make the changes in their life to allow them to live their dream. Questions the PEOPLE Model™ practitioner might ask the individual might include:

- Where do you feel that you "own" your life?

- Tell me how you see yourself being responsible for the things that happen to you.

- How is being accountable important to the decisions you make, and their outcomes?

- How does being responsive relate to the things that happen to you?

- How could you be more responsible?

- How could you be more accountable?

- How could you be more responsive?

- How would your life change if you were more responsible?

- How would your life change if you were more accountable?

- How would your life change if you were more responsive?

Whether an individual is striving to improve his or her life in general, get hold of his or her finances, improve self-esteem, relate better to the people around them, or any number of issues that people generally see life coaches about, these are incredibly powerful questions that will allow people to seriously think about how ownership and taking responsibility affects their lives. With thoughtful, good answers to these questions in hand, the participant can identify areas that need to be changed in order to live the best life possible. Once the areas are identified the individual can explore ways of effecting change, come up with a road map, and then facilitate changes to make goals a reality.

Possibilities

A PEOPLE Model™ practitioner working with a business might ask the following questions under the Possibilities element:

- What do you see the benefits of exploring possibilities for the future are?

- If you did not do what you do, what else could be achieved by this business (using the premises, equipment, machinery, people, or resources)?

- What else might your customers want you to do for them?

- How is creativity encouraged?

- How else could you suggest changes or improvements?

- What else could you do to enhance suggestions?

- What does continuous improvement mean here?

- How brave is the business in its future plans?

Using the same model, but different questions, a PEOPLE Model™ practitioner who is also a small business advisor could help a young entrepreneur bring his sole-proprietorship business from fledgling to full-on success. Some questions the PEOPLE Model™ practitioner might ask include:

- Why is exploring future possibilities important to you?

- Using your skills, resources, and training, what else could you offer to your customers through your business that you are not already offering?

- What are some additional needs of your market?

- What are you passionate about, and how can you incorporate this into your business?

- How do you stay creative?

- Given the right resources, education, and knowledge, where can you envision your business going?

- What are your dreams for your business? What do you need to turn your dreams into a reality?

- When it comes to future plans how brave are you?

These powerful questions will help the young entrepreneur avoid any ruts when it comes to his business. Thinking about what's possible for the young company—and coming up with solutions to make those dreams a reality—will ensure that the entrepreneur grows his business in the right direction. Dreaming, creativity, and passion have an important place in the business world as well as in life, and the right questions can motivate you to action to make your dreams a reality.

Linkage

A PEOPLE Model™ practitioner working with a business might ask the following questions under the Linkage element:

- How do you align business/team/department/personal goals?

- How could you improve this?

- What does the business/team/department/individual want?

- How do you know this?

- What does the business/team/department/individual need?

- How do you know?

- Are they the same?

- How can you link them?

- What surprises you about this?

- What makes the business/team/department/individual happy?

- How do you know?

- What surprises you about this?

Using the same model but different questions, you could inspire just about any kind of group, from associations and boards to sports teams, and even individuals. As an example, we are going to use a tennis team in which the participants compete individually. While the team competes as a whole, individuals are also concerned with their personal performance as well as their status on the team. How do you link the two together? The PEOPLE Model™ practitioner might ask questions like:

- How do you currently align the team's goals with the goals of the individuals on the team?

- What are the team's goals?

- What are individual goals?

- Are these the same?

- How can you link them?

- What makes the team as a whole happy?

- What makes the individuals happy?

- How do you know?

- Can you link them?

Asking these kinds of questions brings to light the goals of the team as a whole versus the goals of the individuals on the team. It brings to light the fact that the goals of one are different from the goals of the other. The questions inspire them to think about how they can link the goals of the team as a whole and the goals of the individuals together. Again, the model for a sports team is no different than the model for a business. The only difference lies in the specific questions that are asked.

Evidence

A PEOPLE Model™ practitioner working with a business might ask the following questions under the Evidence element:

- How do you know when it's worth doing what you do?

- What evidence do you have?

- What other evidence might you find?

- How do you validate the value of time or financial investments?

- How do you measure Return on Investment?

- How do teams and individuals validate the value of time or financial investment?

- Describe the culture here.

- What would you like changed?

- How could it be improved?

- How are the organizations/teams/departments performing in relation to your goals?

Again, the PEOPLE Model™ is non-prescriptive. Let's say a PEOPLE Model™ practitioner who is also a life coach is working with a person who is giving serious consideration to the career he or she has chosen. Some questions the PEOPLE Model™ practitioner might ask would be:

- How can you tell if your job is meaningful to you?

- What evidence do you have that your job is meaningful?

- What benchmarks do you use to determine whether or not your job is right for you? Financial? Security? Passion? Enjoyment?

- What evidence do you have that shows your job is meeting these benchmarks?

- What would you change about your career?

- How could you improve your job?

- What are your goals in life (financial, personal, etc.), and how is your job helping you meet them?

- What evidence do you have?

The questions allow the person contemplating their career path to think about how their career is meeting their needs, or how it can better meet their needs, based on evidence.

By now you should understand that the PEOPLE Model™ is not just for businesses. While it is certainly the perfect resource for any business looking to improve and function at its optimal level, the PEOPLE Model™ is also perfect for groups or individual people. Sports teams, individuals looking to improve an aspect of their lives, associations, volunteer foundations, and boards—the PEOPLE Model™ is for all of them.

Any group or individual who uses the model can expect the following:

1. Support from a PEOPLE Model™ practitioner, using a diagnostic tool such as Perception Gap, Task Coaching, or Development Wheels.

2. Once the issue is properly identified, the group or individual is inspired to think about, and change, the issue through a series of powerful questions that fall under the six elements that make up the PEOPLE Model™. While the model does not change the questions do, and this is what makes the PEOPLE Model™ so versatile.

3. Once the group or individual has been inspired by the questions, they explore ways in which they can meet their goals.

4. Once they find a way to meet their goals, they put their plan into action. This is the facilitation part of the process, which takes the plan and makes it into reality.

5. A culture that promotes positive change and continual improvement for the group or individual is the end result.

4

Three Examples: A Business, A Sports Team, An Individual

To further show the non-prescriptive nature of the PEOPLE Model™, let's take three very different entities—a business, a sports team, and an individual—and let's show what their experience using the PEOPLE Model™ might be.

It must be said that there is no "typical" company, group, or individual designed to fit into the model. As a matter of fact, there is probably no "typical" company, group, or individual! The issues and problems that each entity faces—the barriers that prevent them from reaching optimal success—will be unique to that group. And the PEOPLE Model™ is designed to uncover and unblock any type of barrier. The examples below are merely examples of barriers that an entity may be encountering. Your barriers may be similar, or they may be quite different.

A Business

A PEOPLE Model™ practitioner is called in to help a manufacturing company get back on track. While management can't quite put their finger on what is wrong, the company is unable to keep up with the production and output of their competitors.

Using the Development Wheel as a diagnostic tool, the practitioner helps the people within the company realize that certain organizational changes need to be made in order to fill in certain gaps that will help the performance of the company increase.

Using inspirational questions, the practitioner leads the group in a discussion about how the company is currently organized, as well as how organizational change may affect the company. In a three-stage process devoted to the topic of organizational change, the group analyzes the gap between the company's present state and the company's desired state.

During the second part of the process, the practitioner helps the group explore ways in which the desired result can be reached. Certain milestones along the route are discussed, and questions may be asked regarding skill set, education, learning, and resources.

Finally, the group will talk about how they are going to manage the process of change. This is a very important part of the exercise. Remember, change can never be taken lightly, and it is often difficult for workers—particularly workers who have been at a company for a significant amount of time—to adapt to new methods. Talking about how the process is going to be managed and including everyone involved handles the emotional side of change, which should never be ignored.

A Sports Team

The state swim team is posed to head for the National championship, but despite excellent swimmers and a great season, morale is low. The coach wants to figure out what is causing the breakdown, and also wants to motivate his swimmers, as a team, to go out and win the championship. So he calls in a PEOPLE Model™ practitioner to help things along.

Using the diagnostic tool called Task Coaching, the team lists issues of trust as its primary barrier. The players don't often trust the coach to make the right decisions when it comes to who he chooses to compete, and since the players to some degree must compete against each other for the prime spots on the team, they don't often trust each other.

Under the Ownership element, the PEOPLE Model™ practitioner leads a conversation using inspiring questions related to accountability, responsibility, and responsiveness.

Using a tool called the Fairness model, the practitioner helps the team determine the reasons for the mistrust, and together the group decides to put certain actions into place to rectify the situation.

The group also engages in something called a "trust tower." The trust tower shows how each individual contributes to the team.

Building trusts goes hand-in-hand with motivation, and also factors into the culture of the team. As trust in each other grows, a huge barrier to performance recedes.

The Individual

An individual calls in a life coach to improve the overall direction of her life. She has noticed that most of her endeavors—career, family, hobbies, finances—fall short of her goals and expectations. The life coach, also a licensed PEOPLE Model™ practitioner, uses the diagnostic tool called Task Coaching to determine barriers. The practitioner also does something called the H.A.B.E. exercise to look at invisible barriers as they relate to habits, attitudes, beliefs, and expectations.

The diagnostic tools show that the individual has a commitment gap. In this particular situation, there is a difference in the motivation and confidence that the individual possesses, versus the motivation and confidence that the individual needs to possess in order to meet her goals and live life to the fullest.

Under the Possibilities element, a series of questions are asked that inspire the individual to explore ways that she can make changes that will improve both her motivation and her confidence.

Ways to make improvements are explored; a plan is put into place designed to help her reach her goals when it comes to family, career, finances, and hobbies.

5

How the PEOPLE Academy has used the PEOPLE Model™: A Real Case Study

There is no better evidence of the success of the PEOPLE Model™ than the PEOPLE Academy itself. Yes, it just stands to reason that we've used the PEOPLE Model™ every step of the way as we've created our business. Here's how we've used each element of the Model to create, grow, and ensure success for our business.

PERFORMANCE

In our first conversation, what did we talk about? We talked about what good looked like, at the time, for each of our individual businesses. We then compared what good looked like to what good COULD look like if we pooled our knowledge and experience.

The Performance element was tested during the first meeting between the three of us, when we met in person to share our skills, knowledge, and experience to further define the current good.

And we continued to use the Performance element as we traveled between countries, determining what good might look like in the future for the PEOPLE Academy. The Performance element was one of the most important elements to the building of our business. It took a lot of time and soul-searching, but using the PEOPLE Model™ we eventually determined what good looks like for the PEOPLE Academy. We had a mission and a goal!

How We Used the Performance Element
- We compared what good currently looked like for our individual companies.

- We discussed seeing a bigger and better good by getting together and exploring.

- We met many times over the course of a long period of time to determine what good looked like in the future for the PEOPLE Academy.

EFFICACY

Using the Efficacy element, we determined what skills we had, and how we could use them to achieve our new good.

It was equally important to discover where our skills gaps were. In order to reach our goals we would have to identify our areas of weakness and bolster them! Using the same diagnostic tools and exercises that are now available to all PEOPLE Model™ practitioners, we identified a skill gap in getting to larger networks, as well as a blockage when it came to our database of contacts. Once these issues were identified we worked to resolve them.

It's also worth noting that the Efficacy element really drove home our belief in the PEOPLE Model™, as well as our team esteem. And these things would turn out to be so important! Our belief and team esteem was so strong that it kept us at the table even through the low times that every growing business experiences.

How We Used the Efficacy Element
- We identified our skills, and decided how we would use them to achieve our goals.

- Using diagnostic tools, we identified skill gaps that needed to be filled in order to achieve our goals.

- We developed a strong belief in our mission and team esteem.

OWNERSHIP

The Ownership element was one of the most prevalent elements along our journey to establishing the PEOPLE Academy and the PEOPLE Model™.

Along the way we constantly discussed accountability, responsibility, and responsiveness. As a matter of fact, hardly a decision was made regarding the venture without discussing who was accountable, who was responsible, and who was responsive. And how did this help us? It gave us all a clear picture of what we expected from ourselves, as well as what the others on the team expected of us. Remember, whether you are a business, a sports team, or an individual with goals, you must have a clear understanding of the role you play in meeting those goals.

How We Used the Ownership Element
- Along our journey we decided upon accountability.

- Along our journey we decided upon responsibility.

- Along our journey we decided upon responsiveness.

POSSIBILITIES

The Possibilities element is certainly one of the most fun elements. At least we thought so! Remember, the Possibilities element allows you to dream about what is possible, and then formulate an action plan to turn those possibilities into realities. The Possibilities element allows you to unleash your creativity. All three of us are creative people, so we really enjoyed using this element!

How did we use it? Specifically, we spent a lot of time dreaming about and then talking about bringing the PEOPLE Model™ and all its opportunities to the United States, Europe, Australasia, and the rest of the world.

We also talked about possible targets for the PEOPLE Model™, and decided that it would appeal to coaches (business, life, and sports), consultants, human resources personnel, managers, and other leaders.

And how would we get the word out about the PEOPLE Model™. Again, we had to get creative! We decided that using agents, developing an online presence, and writing this very book would be a great way to spread the word about the PEOPLE Model™.

Once we determined what was possible, we put an action plan into place to make sure that all those possibilities became reality!

How We Used the Possibilities Element
- We considered what was possible when it came to opportunities with the PEOPLE Model™.

- We considered what was possible when it came to who our potential customers would be.

- We considered what was possible in terms of spreading the word about the PEOPLE Model™.

- We turned those possibilities into an action plan, so those dreams can become reality.

LINKAGE

Under the Linkage element, we thought about how what we were doing linked to the overall picture. Specifically, how did what we were doing contribute to our overall goals?

This was an important element for us in particular. Why? Because as we built our business, we were also involved in our previous businesses. It was a scary and difficult decision, but during our Linkage phase we decided that in order to meet our goals with the PEOPLE Model™, we would stop trading in our other businesses. It was not easy to turn clients down, but we knew that we had to do so in order to concentrate on building the PEOPLE Academy. After much soul-searching, we realized that trading was not serving to meet our goals.

Instead, we kept our focus in the development stage by only doing what did serve our goals. And we worked on urgent and important stuff first.

How We Used the Linkage Element
- We talked about how our current actions were linked to our future goals.

- We decided to stop trading with our other businesses, in order to concentrate on meeting our goals for the PEOPLE Academy.

- We focused only on those things that served to help us meet our goals.

EVIDENCE

The Evidence element can be very rewarding—and telling!

After the PEOPLE Model™ was up and running we were able to determine whether or not our goals were being met by looking at certain evidence.

And at the end of the day, we decided that we had a great product! It seemed we had an overwhelmingly positive response to the PEOPLE Model™ (and you can check out Chapter Eight if you are interested in what others have to say about the PEOPLE Model™) from all kinds of business, personal, economic development, practitioner, and partner development levels.

Of course, the Evidence element can also tell you when something has gone awry. And we're not perfect! In our case, there was evidence that our web site just wasn't working. People were confused by it, and many just couldn't get a clear understanding of what the PEOPLE Model™ was through our web site.

So what did we do? We changed our web site.

We still use the Evidence element to continually monitor our decisions and whether or not what we are doing is working. And we'll continue to do so.

So where do we go from here? Well, the rest, as they say, is future history! However, the PEOPLE Academy is only as strong as the three people behind it. And we're sure to face the same issues and problems that all other groups, teams, and individuals face. To that end, we see ourselves continuing to test our product in our own search to grow, improve, and meet our goals.

Toni Reece, Neil Annis, and Linda Harland 43

How We Used the Evidence Element

• We gauged everyone's reaction to our product. Overwhelming consensus? It's a great product!

• We found evidence that our web site wasn't helping us meet our goals, so we changed it.

• We'll continue to look for evidence that supports our business is meeting its goals.

6

Frequently Asked Questions

Q: What is the PEOPLE Academy, and what do they do?

A: A new international business with offices in the UK, USA, and Australasia.

The PEOPLE Academy was formed by the coming together of two organizations to merge the skills, knowledge, and experience of the founding partners. Together, we designed the PEOPLE Model™. The PEOPLE Academy saw a need for growth and development in performance coaching, as we felt that none of the existing models that are used as industry standards gave a fully comprehensive tool that could easily be applied in a business focused context.

So what was the aim? To develop a sophisticated, logical, and impacting international model that could provide a practical people-focused approach to performance improvement.

The PEOPLE Academy created and owns the PEOPLE Model™. Its mission is to roll out its application across the world by training and developing a global network of highly sought after PEOPLE Model™ accredited practitioners.

Q: What is the PEOPLE Model™?

A: Well, hopefully you have a good idea after reading this far! In a nutshell, the PEOPLE Model™ is a performance coaching model based on things that work. It is a framework and road map to running a successful organization through its people.

The PEOPLE Model™ is a strategy, as well as a language for focusing improvement activities with clients. It's logical, makes sense, and is a step-by-step approach to coaching business success. Using the PEOPLE Model™ you will begin to identify and improve key areas of performance within your organization, including: planning, leadership, management, team members, managing performance, barriers to performance, training and development, evaluating training and development, motivation, ownership, building trust, continuous improvement, possibilities, managing change, communication skills, assertive behaviors, recruitment and selection, and action planning.

Q: Who would use the PEOPLE Model™?

A: The two key audiences for working with the PEOPLE Model™ are:

People working with a business, team, or organization to provide support and help it grow:

- Experienced coaches

- Consultants

- Trainers

- Practitioners

- Business Advisors

People working within a business driving its growth:

- HR people

- Leaders

- Managers

- Team leaders

- Department heads

- Supervisors

Q: How is the PEOPLE Model™ different from using other consultants?

A: The difference between the PEOPLE Model™ and other approaches is that some consultant approaches are process driven and people dragged. It is often seen that the consultant tells them what is wrong and they need to put it right. The PEOPLE Model™ is, as it says, people focused. It relies on the knowledge of the people within the organization and works closely with those who do the jobs. It engages the workforce in order to build a better business or organization. The people in the organization collectively set the criteria for what good looks like, which gains buy-in from the start and helps with collaborative working between management and staff to improve the situation and work toward improvement.

Q: How would someone using the PEOPLE Model™ diagnose the needs of an organization they are working with.

A: As well as creating a PEOPLE Model™, the PEOPLE Academy has developed a number of approaches to identifying organizational and individual needs. These are practical, effective, and best of all, easy to use!

These include:

- Task Coaching Sessions. These are coaching sessions focused on an individual or team to identify what gets in the way of good performance.

- Perception Gap. Perception Gap is an online staff survey that seeks input from everyone on what works well and what works less well in their organization. Perception Gap produces a significant report from input provided by staff for leaders to review with their PEOPLE Model™ practitioner.

- Development Wheels. This diagnostic tool allows clients to rate satisfaction in several different areas, and identifies areas that need to be worked on. The exercise also allows those involved to understand the skills and attributes needed to fill the gaps.

All of these diagnostic tools can be used in individual coaching sessions, in group sessions, on the phone, or face-to-face.

Q: What are the benefits to a business, team, or organization using the PEOPLE Model™?

A: Through the PEOPLE Model™, an organization will be steered by its leaders while being driven by its people. It is a clear strategy for business performance improvement which business leaders identify with and want to work with. The strategies of the PEOPLE Model™ mine deeper into the heart of a business in order to drive future business success more effectively.

Q: What does the PEOPLE Academy system offer?

A: The PEOPLE Academy licenses others to use the PEOPLE Model™ and its related material, which include:

- The diagnostic tools

- The PEOPLE Model™ presentation

- The PEOPLE Model™ resources manual

- Online support

- Tutorials

- The ability to download resources and templates as needed

- A service that allows you to "ask the expert" about particular situations

As an added bonus, all PEOPLE Model™ practitioners are listed on the PEOPLE Academy web site.

PART II
The Licensed Practitioner

7

Why Become a Licensed PEOPLE Model™ Practitioner?

Glad you asked! If you deal with people, whether you are external to a business or organization or on the inside of one, your goal is most likely to inspire people, explore potential, and facilitate results. And that is exactly what the PEOPLE Model™ does. The opportunities for a practitioner to gain new clients or work with existing clients using the PEOPLE Model™ have no boundaries. After all, the founders of the PEOPLE Academy and co-creators of the PEOPLE Model™ have used these concepts to help others succeed for a collective 50 years. The PEOPLE Model™ comprises the best resources possible to address many different business challenges. As we've mentioned several times throughout this book, the model is non-prescriptive and allows the practitioner to tailor its use in the best way for themselves and their clients. The PEOPLE Model™ works in all types and sizes of business, organizations, teams, associations, boards—basically wherever you can find people themselves! Simply stated, the PEOPLE Model™ is a complete business!

Listed below are just a few of the benefits of using the PEOPLE Model™ with clients:

- The PEOPLE Model™ is a clear strategy for growth, whether your client is a business, a sports team, an individual, or an organization.

- The PEOPLE Model™ translates easily between practitioners, leaders, managers, and teams.

- The PEOPLE Model™ has a proven track record for providing long-term fee-based relationships between the organization and the practitioner.

- The PEOPLE Model™ can be used to obtain new clients by providing a powerful framework at the highest level of the business for organizational development.

- The PEOPLE Model™ can be used with existing clients to drive deeper into the heart of the organization.

- The PEOPLE Model™ is owned by the PEOPLE Academy, and only licensed practitioners can use it with clients, giving both parties the edge over the competitors. However, PEOPLE Model™ practitioners are licensed to work with all kinds of business and organizations, or all sizes and in all sectors. The license does not restrict practitioners' activities with clients in any part of the world, and allows the practitioner freedom to trade wherever they wish.

The PEOPLE Model™ and its supporting resources are a significant addition to the portfolio of any coach, consultant, or advisor, manager, human resource professional, or leader.

The business and life coaching systems have been designed and refined by the founders of the PEOPLE Academy and is the fruit of their 50 years collective practical experience.

Best of all, everything provided is tried, tested, and really works!

As we mentioned before, our customers fall into two categories. The first category are those customers who are external to a business or organization:

- Experienced coaches

- Consultants

- Trainers

- Practitioners

- Business Advisors

- Business Leaders

- Franchise Training Centers

- Employer Training Centers

- Career Redirection

What does the above group have in common, you ask? Well, regardless of the stage of client activity in which they engage, the above list of potential practitioners have one thing in common—they all deal with people. They inspire people, explore potential, and facilitate results.

So what makes up our second category of customers? There are many customers who would use the PEOPLE Model™ internal to a business. This category includes:

- Human Resource personnel

- Leaders/managers

- Team leaders

- Department heads

- Supervisors

We like to refer to our customers within a business as the "internal champions." These individuals inspire employees at all levels every day. They are called on for their advice and guidance. They explore all possibilities of a challenge to make improvements, and they facilitate the process of improvement flawlessly. These are the people who are making a difference every day in companies and organizations all over the world. The Internal champions and the PEOPLE Model™ are the perfect fit!

So, as you are thinking about whether or not being a PEOPLE Model™ practitioner is right for you and your business, we bet you are wondering what makes the model different from other offerings on the market. We are so glad you asked! For those supporting a business, the PEOPLE Model™ differs from other offerings because instead of just giving you training, an idea, or concept, it provides coaches and consultants with a complete business. You'll learn:

- How to get clients

- How to satisfy their needs

- How to create and maintain long-term fee-based relationships

- How to enjoy status as an accredited PEOPLE Model™ practitioner.

You should know that for those within an organization, the PEOPLE Model™ provides a complete performance improvement strategy.

The PEOPLE Model™ may be used by licensed practitioners only. Not everyone can trade with it, or use its methodology. The PEOPLE Model™ is a trademark of the PEOPLE Academy!

So, how do you know if you have the correct skills to be a PEOPLE Model™ practitioner? Well, the PEOPLE Academy suggests that any potential practitioner has a fundamental appreciation of what's involved in running a business or organization. We also suggest that licensed PEOPLE Model™ practitioners are comfortable dealing with people at all levels in a business or organization, and it's helpful if they are skilled in coaching, consulting, or managing.

The Manuals

We've already mentioned some of the things that the license includes, like an orientation, unlimited support, and practitioner manuals. We wanted to talk a bit more about the business and life coaching manuals, which are comprehensive and include just about anything a PEOPLE Model™ practitioner is likely to encounter.

First of all, the manuals are an excellent resource for anyone who wants to truly understand the PEOPLE Model™. The roles and responsibilities of both the practitioners and the participants are made very clear, and the art of facilitation is discussed in detail. Action planning is covered extensively in the business planning manual, and there are a large and varied amount of templates and exercises to use with the model included. Other topics that the manuals cover in detail include:

- Business planning

- Life improvement

- How to determine what good looks like

- Leadership

- What makes a good manager

- Developing people

- Performance management

- Barriers to performance training and development

- Evaluating training

- Motivation

- Building trust

- The concept of continuous improvement

- How to find possibilities

- Managing change

- Communication

- Assertive behaviors

- Recruitment and selection

- Gaining business

The manual also explains the three main diagnostic tools you've heard us talk a lot about in this book. These diagnostic tools are the Development Wheels, which allow you to identify gaps in areas of your business; Task Coaching, which allows you to identify and come up with solutions to barriers to performance; and an online survey called the Perception Gap, which allows senior managers, managers, and staff to record their input about where they perceive issues to be within the organization.

So, now that you know all about becoming a licensed PEOPLE Model™ practitioner, what is the next step? Getting in touch, of course! Please check out our web site at www.ThePeopleAcademy.com, or feel free to contact us at Info@ThePeopleAcademy.com or at one of our three offices:

USA

Email: Toni@ThePeopleAcademy.com

Europe

Email: Neil@ThePeopleAcademy.com

Australasia

Email: Linda@ThePeopleAcademy.com

8

What Others Have to Say About the PEOPLE Model™

"We are so confident that this model is the future of business coaching we are willing to endorse and recommend it to all our coaches and to people already coaching within companies."
The Coaching Academy—Europe's largest coaching training provider

"The PEOPLE model™ is revolutionary—it will make life easier as an HR professional, but will also allow us to create a more focused, happier team."
Ann Wilkes—HR Director

"One of the most innovative approaches to performance coaching today. It's a must-have for anybody remotely interested in the coaching profession, because it will take coaches from where they are today to where they will need to be tomorrow. The coaching profession is continually evolving and expanding at a rapid pace. You have to keep up or be left behind."
Terry Levine, PhD., MCC., CEO Comprehensive Coaching U
Speaker and Best-Selling Author of *Work Yourself Happy*

"The PEOPLE model™ is the fastest way to get results from people—I highly recommend it."
M. Watkins—Training Manager

"Excellent."
M. A. North London

"When the PEOPLE model™ was explained to me I fell in love with its simplicity and effectiveness. This is certainly the way forward in my business."
Mike Chantel—Executive Coach

"The material was wonderful and well presented."
Ballu Patel

"I am so please I did this course, I can't tell you.

I have introduced the PEOPLE model™ to five people already and with all five had extremely positive responses. One has asked me to present at a seminar and another is considering me to work with their whole team.

You really imparted an enormous amount of information, energy and experience.

I am so pleased I took the decision to "just do it"—my mind is buzzing with plenty of ideas."
Ben Leon

"Exceeded expectations!

A really good product that brings together many tools and suggested ways of working in one place. I haven't come across this before."
Michaela Partridge

"Like many new coaches, I came our of my certification program with a lot of great knowledge and a ton of enthusiasm. After years of searching for a fulfilling career, I had finally found my passion and was eager to begin my life on this new path. What I quickly discovered, however, was that while I had all of the "people" skills necessary to be a life coach, what I lacked was a structured and organized way of coaching—a real program to take my clients through that would bring about the best results for them. I resigned myself to the fact that I would either have to create my own resources from scratch (and not knowing where to even begin) or find a viable solution.

While searching for this solution, I found the PEOPLE Model™. This program has given me phenomenal tools and resources to use with my clients, in a structured format that works with any issue that my clients may be facing. The online tutorials included with the model are invaluable, providing additional explanations and insights into how the model works. I now have a solid foundation for coaching my clients, which also gives me added confidence when talking about coaching to prospective new clients and people I meet every day. Being able to explain that I use the PEOPLE Model™ as a basis of my life coaching, with a short explanation of how it works, makes selling my coaching services so much easier. It also adds the degree of professionalism that I've been looking for in promoting the benefits of life coaching.

I highly recommend the PEOPLE Model™ for use in any life coaching business. Whether a coach has been in the business for a while or just completing their certification, it will certainly give them a competitive edge and some life-changing tools and resources that will propel their clients forward. And especially for those just beginning their life coaching practice, it absolutely answers that first scary question of "Where do I start?"
Deb Britt
Spiral Path Coaching

"Your energy and enthusiasm were infectious and I am still buzzing with it all!

The PEOPLE model™ is a fabulous concept, all tried and tested material, but what a difference to have it all packaged within a structure that makes perfect business sense and saves you months if not years of searching and gathering the right tools.

The PEOPLE Model™ is just a fabulous business structure to take a business through if it wishes to improve."
Elena Dickie

"I thought it was brilliant."
Catherine Usher

"The standard and the applicability of the PEOPLE Model™ diagnostic tools and resource manuals are high."
Colin Clark

"I am sure the PEOPLE Model™ will work wonders for us all."
Neil Jenner

About the PEOPLE Academy

The PEOPLE Academy is an international business with offices in the United States, the United Kingdom and New Zealand.

The PEOPLE Academy is a coming together of two businesses: Baysix Training, Inc., of the United States, and People & Business in Mind Ltd. of the United Kingdom.

The PEOPLE Academy founders realized that, based on years of experience with direct client engagement, there was a missing piece in business that would connect people better with their organizations. The missing element was a universal performance coaching system, or road map, that could be easily understood and implemented by all levels and all types of businesses.

The aim of the PEOPLE Academy was to create a powerful, impacting business development tool—the PEOPLE Model™.

About the Authors

Toni Reece

Toni Reece has spent more than 15 years in the Quality Assurance Industry prior to creating Baysix Training Inc. in 1995. In addition to being the first trained practitioner in the United States for the international people development model, Investors in People, her previous experience includes: Manager of Customer Quality for an international battery manufacturer, Director of Continuous Quality Improvement, ISO-9000 Lead Auditor, technical skills in documentation and work flow process in concert with a highly passionate ability to work with people at all levels of the organization. As comfortable on the shop floor as she is in the board room, Toni has developed and implemented a variety of people-centered solutions to performance improvement issues including:

- Coaching and mentoring

- Employee-driven task assessments

- Process improvement

- Internal customer/supplier awareness

- Design of Outrageous Customer Care

- Visual method sheet development

- Corrective action design and training

- Facilitation training

- Leadership training

- Corporate team building

- Performance management

- Supervisor development

Toni Reece resides in the United States and is passionate about facilitating the power of the individual.

And here are Toni's three Golden Business Rules:

1. Authenticity—Always remain genuine and real when dealing with others.

2. Integrity—Behave at all times with the utmost honesty and fairness when dealing with others.

3. Passion—Remain passionate within and about the business or get out!

Neil Annis

Neil has more than 20 years experience in operational management, sales, change management, training and coaching, and personal and organizational development. His experiences include:

- Attitude shift

- Business networking

- Change management

- Coaching

- Contract management

- Facilitation

- Goal setting

- Investment in excellence

- Marketing

- NLP Master Practitioner Business

- Operational management

- Presenting

- Public speaking

- Sales

- Team working

- Training and development

- Training needs analysis

Neil resides in the United Kingdom. His three Golden Business Rules are:

1. Be authentic

2. Be progressive.

3. Never lose sight of why you are working—keep it real!

Linda Harland

Linda is a practical Human Resource and Training Consultant with 20 years experience in management development and people management comprising:

- Life coaching

- Performance coaching

- Master NLP business practitioner

- Transactional analysis

- Investment in excellence

- Behavioral competencies

- Recruitment and selection

- Assessment centers

- Absence management

- Conflict resolution

- Personal effectiveness

- Managing people

- Managing performance

- Change management

- Attitude shift

Born in Edinburgh and now living in New Zealand, Linda is dedicated to the development and recognition of peoples' potential.

She has a strong business background and has worked with a range of companies from blue-chip organizations to owner-run businesses, and is passionate in ensuring the growth of people to improve their success.

Linda's Three Golden Business Rules are:

1. Treat people fairly and with respect.

2. Believe in what you say.

3. Do what you do because you want to, not because you have to.

978-0-595-42841-0
0-595-42841-X

www.ingramcontent.com/pod-product-compliance
Lightning Source LLC
Chambersburg PA
CBHW021004180526
45163CB00005B/1882